The World is Waking Up:

Poetry of Resistance from Youth Around the World

Edited by Jason Ryberg and Clara Rabbani,
Artwork by Clara Rabbani

Kansas City   Spartan Press   Missouri

Spartan Press
Kansas City, MO
spartanpresskc.com

Copyright ©, 2019
First Edition 1 3 5 7 9 10 8 6 4 2
ISBN: 978-1-950380-57-2
LCCN: 2019948248

Design, edits and layout: Jason Ryberg, Clara Rabbani
Cover image: Clara Rabbani
All rights reserved. No part of this publication may be reproduced or transmitted in any form or by any means, electronic or mechanical, including photocopying, recording or by info retrieval system, without prior written permission from the author.

Acknowledgments

I am indebted to the members of the Social Justice Program at the Pembroke Hill School for reviewing and judging the submissions to the International Poetry of Resistance Contest. Their careful and diligent work made this collection possible.

The leadership and unconditional support of Maud Muscat as the coordinator of the Social Justice program, was fundamental for the completion of this project. I am deeply grateful to her.

I am thankful to slam poetry world champion, Joaquin Zihuatanejo, and author Taylane Cruz for dedicating their time to helping us select the winners of the Contest. My dear friend, poet Annie Newcomer, also helped judge the contest and has lovingly encouraged me throughout the years to write and explore poetry.

My English teacher, Ben Christian, was of invaluable help supervising my year long research on Poetry of Resistance. His insight, support and guidance accompanied me from beginning to end.

The illustrations in this book are the result of the time I spent in Chandra Ramey´s art class. Her thoughtful critique has pushed me forward always.

This book would not be possible without the vision of Jason Ryberg at Spartan Press and his willingness to invest in this project.

Finally, and most importantly, I must acknowledge the hundreds of youth from around the world who were willing to share their love, indignation and hope through the vessel of poetry.

TABLE OF CONTENTS

Introduction / Clara Rabbani

Joanna Lau / Between Dawn and Indigo / 1

Krishi Desai / Fruit Fly Thoughts / 3

Dominique Cuningkin / Riddle Me (Self) Love / 5

Ava Minu-Sepehr / Baba in my dream / 6

Priscila Oliveira Nascimento / Arma das minorias / 10

Laila Carter / What a Black Woman Tastes Like / 12

Rachel Otero / Impact / 14

Joss Aiken / Hiding from Monsters / 17

Ileana Viridiana Romero López / En Este Momento / 20

Augustus Hoff / Elements / 22

Katherine Kallas / The Worst Generation / 25

Somya Wadhwa / Kill Your Darlings / 27

Chloe Jane Rosenstock / Thanksgiving / 30

Joss Aiken / Manipulate / 32

Shivani Deshmukh / I Am A Women / 34

Sidra Nizami / I am a firework / 37

Sophia Gotham / Fly On / 38

Elianna Lee / seven words of advice to a conflicted friend / 39

William Graham / Moonlight Man / 40

Katherine Kallas / Beauty is Pain / 44

Narine Verdiyan / Fell in love with Lonely / 46

Minerva Macarrulla / I Tell Everyone Who Asks That The Reason My Phone Is Entirely In Spanish Is Because It Helps Me Learn Faster; Closer To The Truth Is That It Helps Me Remember / 49

Nataly Kazzi / like the sky holds its shining stars / 51

Ashley Kim / Foreign Tongues / 55
Jasmine Li / System Error: Shutdown Imminent / 57
Bhagyashree Barman / The World's Waking Up / 59
Rayna Bowman / See me / 62
Ava Minu-Sepehr / Nastaran (the love song) / 64
Katherine Kallas / Drugged Dream / 66
R'keria Davis / Possession of a Smell / 67
Rayna Bowman / Envy / 68
Dominique Cuningkin / Individualism / 70
Molly Duke / Grab Her / 71
Katherine Kallas / Grim Reaper in the High School / 73
Rehma Khan / The impervious hue of hope / 76
Rialin Yasay / The Drought / 79
Ava Minu-Sepehr / I can't go there now / 82
Taylor Drummer / Drugs Money Women / 84
Drizzle Bayer / Quiet Your Mind / 85
Mion Charity / beauty lies / 88
Rayna Bowman / Revelation / 89
Minerva Macarrulla / Thawing / 90
Dana Abou-Diab / Pride! / 91
Elizabeth Bowling / Humiliation / 94
Elizabeth Bowling / If I Ever . . . / 97
Katie Vandermel / The Gay Rose / 100
Thayse Souza dos Santos Santos / Mundo Revirado / 102
Giselly Kamily de Jesus Santos Santos / Tempos Sombrios / 106
Pablo Montalvão / Ritual Poético / 110
Michelle María Gómez Álvarez / Resistir lo cotidiano / 113

Matheus Alves / Um Cordel Pro Valentão. / 117

Paloma Ximena Becerril Ramirez / Miedo / 121

Priscila Oliveira Nascimento / Sementes de luta / 125

Jeanne Lainé / Depuis la nuit des temps / 129

Alexandre Joissains / Indolence opaline / 131

Audry Barré / Resistancialisme / 133

Trudy Pearce / Edited / 135

Faith Victoria / Of a tramp / 137

Natalie Rovello / Making Maps / 139

Hector Manuel Orreaga Ramirez / El sentido de la vida / 140

Alex Perez / The Truth / 142

Contributors / 143

Artwork by Clara Rabbani

Quote Collage / 2

Horses / 9

Gun / 19

Storks / 24

Skeleton / 29

Stippling Face / 36

Beach / 43

Dream / 48

Music / 56

Hands / 61

Migration / 78

Water Crisis / 81

Distorted Reality / 87

Hijab and Hair / 93

Elephant / 96

Child Labor / 99

Random Collage / 112

Bean / 127

Self-portrait / 128

Homeless / 136

Tree Stumps / 138

Introduction by Clara Rabbani

Poetry is not a luxury. It is a vital necessity of our existence -Audre Lorde

From the beginning of time, poems have been smuggled out of prisons, exchanged on battlefields, passed from hand to hand, carved on walls, written in the margins, distributed on street corners, and carried in coat-pockets overseas.

Every culture and generation produce poetry in response to the injustices of its time. Deeply rooted in resilience, the enduring nature of poetry and its ability to capture the struggles of the past can serve as a sustaining force in a sea of turmoil. If creativity is a form of protest, then the poet is the protester. Pablo Neruda saw the power of poets and the remarkable potential of their words: *Earth, people, and poetry are one and the same entity tied together by mysterious subterranean passages. When the earth blooms, the people breath freedom, the poets sing and show the way.*[1]

When poems are gathered together, they form a mighty body that is impossible to constrain, like the sea. Every time a poem touches someone's conscience, like gathering drops, it invites the possibility for action, forming a tempest. Thus, the transformative potential of resistance poetry can serve as a potent antidote against the injustices of the world.

****

Music was the first form of resistance I ever knew. At a time when I had nothing to resist but the sleep that weighed down my eyelids, I soaked in the melodies of Chico Buarque and Geraldo Vandré, whose songs challenged the dictatorship in Brazil, and for which they were imprisoned and exiled.

---

[1] Neruda in Eisner, Mark (2018). What We Can Learn from Neruda's *Poetry of Resistance*. *The Daily* (March 26).

They were the disturbers of the world and they captivated me. At a time when I did not yet have a voice with which to speak, I listened to their voices.

In a world where so many are denied a voice, where the right to speak is so readily violated, poetry serves as a unifying force. It draws no boundaries between race, class, religion, or age, and is not limited by languages. Poetry and the truth it holds belong to all. From civil rights in America to women's rights in the Middle East to dictatorships in Latin America, resistance poetry can take many forms against the stains on the pages of history, and, when intended to inspire social change, it can be a sword of resistance.

Poems of protest embody what it means to be alive at a time when our voices are threatened. We live in a fragile, imperfect, and corruptible world. So is not enough to only listen to the words of the poet, but to become the poet, for poetry, like politics, can become corrupt without a diversity of voices and representations.

****

When conceiving the International Poetry of Resistance Contest for youth, which gave birth to this book, I was inspired by the work of many Latin American and Middle Eastern poets. But none was as empowering to me as the life and work of nineteenth century Persian poetess, Táhirih. To those who know her story, she is remembered for speaking the unspeakable, and with her beautiful words and eloquent poetry, inciting resistance against a patriarchal order. Tahirih became one of the first women to receive a diploma and, at the age of fourteen, her fame was already well established as one of the most learned young women of Persia. As an adult, she appeared before an assemblage of men during a conference and throwing off her veil, she proclaimed: *Let us emancipate women and reform society: Let us arise out of our graves of superstition and self,(...) then shall the whole earth respond to freedom of conscience and new life!* Táhirih was eventually captured and executed, but her prophetic last words still ring: *You can kill me as soon as you like but you cannot stop the emancipation of women.*

****

The International Poetry of Resistance Contest, sponsored by the Social Justice Club,[2] had the purpose of empowering youth ages 12 to 18 to capture and express, in the form of poetry, the injustices they face. Through poetry our diversity and interconnectedness could also be embraced and nurtured. Poetry echoes the common struggles of a generation and, in doing so, relieve people's burden of having to suffer alone.

More than two-hundred and fifty poems from twelve countries (Brazil, Mexico, US, Spain, France, England, Ethiopia, Kenya, India, Pakistan, China and the Philippines), and from eighteen American States were submitted and sixty were selected for this book. They reflect resistance in the face of intimate and personal challenges and resistance in the face controversial social issues surrounding freedom of speech and religion, gun violence, the effects of media, gender inequality, and racism. They reveal fears that no other generation had experienced before. As leaders of their generation, these youth yield something far more powerful than the bullets and chains that threaten to puncture and bind them.

---

[2] The Social Justice Club was co-founded by myself and a group of my high school peers at Pembroke Hill School in Kansas City www.sjcinitiative.org. The contest was organized in 2018.

When tyranny darkens the earth and punishes the people, the loudest voice is sought out and the head of the poet falls into history's deep well. Tyranny cuts off the head that sings, but the voice at the bottom of the well returns to the secret springs of the earth and out of the darkness rises up through the mouth of the people (Pablo Neruda).

Poets are the mouthpieces of a peaceful, but not always silent, revolution. That voice at the bottom of the well will always return as long as people are willing to listen. American poet Robert Hass, quoting Bashō, reminds us: *If the horror of the world were the truth of the world, (…) there would be no one to say it/ and no one to say it to.*[3]

While resistance poetry serves the vital purpose of reflecting on the horrors of the world, it also gives voice to the possibilities for greatness embodied in human existence. Neruda's words *You can cut all the flowers, but you cannot stop spring* tell us of those invisible seeds that will bloom in the spring. Poetry is a seed that will never stop growing. Its enduring nature and the variety of experiences that it captures can inspire a long awaited, youthful and beautiful revolution.

Here is the spring and these are its flowers.

****

For as long I can remember, I have been outraged by the way in which we, as humans, treat the environment. We act as if the earth exists only for us while simultaneously believing that we are independent from it. The way our societies are built disregard the natural world and the vital role it plays in our survival. I often ask myself: why do we torture something that gives to us so unconditionally? And why do we expect to still be given afterwards?

---

[3]Sixteen Rivers Press, editor (2018). *America, We Call Your NamePoems of Resistance and Resilience*. Sixteen Rivers Press, San Francisco, California.

"The Lies We Swear Upon", and many of the illustrations in this book, reflect my attempt to make sense of and resist this parasitic relationship.

The Lies We Swear Upon

The earth
is no
Pretty
Little
Thing.

You bind her
and you burn her
and you poison her
with things you cast away.

But when the time comes
for her to cast
You
away,
She will see you
as you are.

She is
Resilient
and she is proud.
She will not deceive you.

And unlike you,
she was made to last–
to outlive you
until you have outlived yourself.

You say
you live
to unearth her secrets,
But she readily
waits.

For,
You cannot conquer
what is already yours;
Oblivious that
you are just as much hers.

She is
the heart of a butterfly.
Delicate.
Every earthquake.
Every storm.
Extraordinary.

She sings to you–
To the beat of the
Pounding
in your chest.

As if you could ignore
the very thing that gave you
Life.

And when she speaks,
She does not
only
Speak.
She roars.

And when she sings,
The very earth you stand on,
Trembles to the rhythm of
Her song.

Once,
You took her whispers
for inconvenience;
Carved from it a mask.
And you forgot that
there is inconvenience
In the truth.

Once,
She held you
to her chest,
And sang.

She put your fingers
to her lips,
And wrapped them in her breathe.

You were hers
just as much as
She was yours.

But the time
for whispers
has passed,
And now she
Roars
for the lions you
Killed.

For the mother
And fathers
you bound in chains.

And for the children,
Whose cries were silenced
by no hand
other than their own.
For, there were no hands left
to silence them
when you came.

And while she trembles
from the sickness that you gave,
To keep her weaker than yourself.
To keep her impotent.
She will not break.
She was not made to break.

Only you
were made that way,
Dear, foolish ones.
Only I was made that way.

So when the storm comes,
And the only one
that ever loved you
more than you loved
Yourself
is gone–
Betrayed.
When she trembles
from the pain,
You will be the first to
Fall.

And there,
On your knees,
You will stay,
With no one left to
Redeem you.

For,
She knows what hides behind
the masks we wear
and the lies we
Swear upon.

The World is Waking Up

To youth everywhere who inspire us to act through the power of their words.

Joanna Lau

Between Dawn and Indigo

The night before eighteen is the tune to a music I won't listen to
anymore because to relive a memory is to lose a part of it

I wake in the afternoon of a lineage of stories and wonder why
dawn shines so brightly outside my window, warm petals fallen

they say we dream in color, but what if cherry blossoms
hint at fading cerulean and murky tangerine paling gray

uncondensed memory dissipates into vapor escaping
the grasp of my fingers—what an injustice to not take it all

in the subway is a drummer pounding down raw cement stairs
replacing curses of old men who have forgotten the color of sunrise

across me sits a man with purple fingernails, coloring
beads in a child's earlobes indigo like wisteria blooming

indigo—the night before eighteen sparkles into dew
rounds the corner and sees that the drummer is a child

Quote Collage

Krishi Desai

Fruit Fly Thoughts

I hear the chattering of a million voices—
Skulls doing the can-can in my head.
They are fruit flies buzzing around,
the ones that are too clever to snap up and kill.
I can't stop those vexatious noises, even when I go 1, 2, 3, relax.
1, 2, 3, breathe. Let it go.
Because there is no sedative for the intangible,
for the fruit flies that have no shape.
They just keep buzzing and buzzing,
drilling away at my tissues and fibers
Even when I wish them away.
Will you be alone forever? You should find someone.
Are you trying hard enough? You should try harder.
And buzz, and buzz.
I douse myself in vinegar and dish soap, but the gnats persist.
The remedies are as useful as handsome proverbs,
failing to cure anything, instead, simply passing the time.
I could slosh in gasoline and drop a match on myself
yet, still, these flies will dance in the inferno,
chanting in their infuriating alto, *Oh silly, silly,*
You can never rid of us!
They feed off of my ineptitude,
my cast-iron ability to botch everything I do,

As they would off of warm honey.
Laying their eggs along the linings of my hippocampus,
    they multiply exponentially
Until they no longer harbor my mind alone:
They take residence in my eyes, in my throat, devouring my lips,
    and shooting out of my mouth.
I am infested,
And there is no longer a cure.

Dominique Cuningkin

Riddle Me (Self) Love

Do me a favor and take time to think
If you harm yourself are you strong or are you weak?
Are you strong because you were able to cause pain,
Or weak because you couldn't take what you gave?

If you thought that was hard, then what about this one:
If you bring yourself down, are you the bully or victim?
Does the harsh words make you the bully,
Or does the pain make you a casualty?

Why do you spend life beating yourself up
When there's so many things about you to love?
You're beautiful, smart, and one of a kind
And you can do anything, when using your mind.

There's no need to worry about what others say
Focus on yourself because that is what pays
You may care for others but love yourself also
Because how can you help if your heart's full of sorrow?

Nobody has the combo of abilities that you do
That comes together perfectly and creates something new
You may be the one to come with an idea
That makes the world better and change how we live.

Ava Minu-Sepehr

Baba in My Dream

Baba
committed suicide in my dream.
many miles away I saw him stand and look at me
he says
I cannot continue, just
no longer needed, and
not worthy.

I saw his
limpid eyes in
yellow light out.
Baba
committed suicide in my dream
removed himself of glowing
felled his own chest.

(Baba)
was still standing but I understood he was not.
Across many deserts I walked, or perhaps stumbled very much
quickly, far more miles than there would have been
slowly, because I will never be that far.
So many people blocked me, called out
my name, but all I heard was *Baba*

(Baba) is now
gone so I must wrap him in blankets, in parenthesis
because he cannot be gone I
shield him, cannot have him take off with such swiftness, I place him and
suicide
on different lines.

Baba,
I am stuck at a crossing of roads,
don't leave me,
left me,
I am coming to you.
Lily and Mama are placed there beside his fallen figure
like two small birch trees, miles away,
when Mama calls me saying

Baba
committed suicide.
He is gone
He is left
and she calls me saying
I cannot survive, I cannot
paint enough colors to save myself.

(Baba)
is gone,
and Mama
is taking herself.

I cry out in such a way, I plead with her to stay
on the phone as I travel a distance too far
I scream out to her.

(Baba)
(Mama)
both gone
the distance so cruel
on different lines
so to prove it is not true
not in this dream,
poem.

Horses

Priscila Oliveira Nascimento

Arma das Minorias

Terra de poucos
Terra do capital
Terra onde o proletário grita por socorro
Neste infeliz sistema brutal

Terra onde minhas irmãs de raça
São covardemente torturadas
E quando finalmente ganham voz
A vida lhes é tirada

Se pensam que podem nos parar
Se pensam que vão nos deter
Sinto muito, estão enganados
A resistência vai ferver

Enquanto houver fôlego
Por igualdade vamos lutar
Não confundam com terrorismo
Nossa arma tem apenas amor pra dar

Priscila Oliveira Nascimento

The Weapon of the Minorities

Land of few
Land of money
Land where the proletarian cries for help
In this unhappy brutal order

Land where my sisters of race
Are cowardly tortured
And when they finally get a voice
Their life is taken away

If they think they can stop us
If they think they're going to detain us
I'm sorry, they're mistaken
Resistance will arise

As long as there is breath
For equality we will fight
Do not confuse with terrorism
Our weapon has only love to offer.

Laila Carter

What a Black Woman Tastes Like

You describe our Skin as
Decadent and Sweet yet
You don't expect our
words to be.

Saccharine Caramel Skin
does not mask too many
ounces of opinion,
more than a pinch of salt
is unpleasant to the tongue
commanding sweetness, but
secretly searching for a
semblance of spice

You describe our Skin as
Chocolates, Toffee's, and Mocha's
however, it is not only our skin
converted into Confectionary
our being, our essence, our black.
Sweet Skin, Savory Words, Black Woman.

Craved Chocolate Skin
made in a cauldron of Cocoa is

already imbedded with bitterness
It is expected, explicit, and enjoyed
You cannot denounce the quiet
rage of the black women
and simultaneously devour
what is delectable.

You describe our Skin as
Butterscotch's, Honey's, and Maple's
We are a commodity
consumed and spat out
when You find us Unsavory
You cannot decide and dilute
flavors you find unpleasant,

things too Sweet
eventually turn
Sour.

Rachel Otero

Impact

wanting to write like
the way oranges were
written into Christmas traditions
like the lady next door
that spoke Spanish to me
even when I didn't understand it
how somehow she knew
my ethnicity was fighting for some air
how the cashier at the gas station
sighed as I pull out my $20 to pay for
my one dollar beverage
but I didn't have the dollar
writing like the way she makes me
feel
complex and misunderstood
making the synapses in my brain
connect to everything around me
words used to explain
the feeling of putting your own hand
on your arm but not knowing
whether it's your hand feeling your arm
or your arm feeling your hand
writing in the second person point of view

telling someone else's story from
your own perspective
the way you see the water at sunset
like it was something being painted in
real time
something admirable and sleepy
writing for my great grandparents
trying to dedicate my pieces to as
many people as I can just so I can have
something left of them when they're gone
writing like how we wouldn't have
shadows without the sun
a downcast past your silver lining
the type of poetry to make
someone smile
grinning ear to ear the way the ocean seems
to if you look really close
how when people die they are never
really gone
the ways we plaster memories
everywhere we go
our footprints dripping in past tense
like the gum you just never remembered
to scrape off your shoe
a burden
lifting weight off your shoulders
sandbags the size of elephants
the way she loved the particular way

you liked to hold her hand
the dimple in your right cheek
everything small and minuscule
that has meaning
I want to write like the way it feels
at the last hello and the first goodbye
needing to leave something
behind
for the earth to take in

Joss Aiken

Hiding from Monsters

Do you remember when I was five,
Soothing me, before bed?
There are no monsters, you are safe, you said.
Do you remember, did you believe that?
Remember the faces of the monsters.
Remember the way they pulled the —

Triggered memories flood to my mind.
I remember, I remember, I remember.
You said I was safe. You said they
Were safe. The them. The many who had monsters
Not under their beds, but in their towns.
Plotting, practicing, polishing the metal of —

The handle of my door is turned and closed.
I remember. I remember. I remember.
Clicking gears, that was what a monster was.
The glowing eyes.
Spittle, teeth, jaws,
Real monsters kill kids in —

School was safe.
There were no beds. No monsters with green horns.

Habitat, noun. The natural home or environment of an animal, plant, or other organism.
Or monster.
They lived in houses, in towns, in states.
Near schools.
Oh, god, they know where the children are.
Protect the children not from their claws but --

Gunning his car, the stranger left.
Something I remembered.
He tried to move quickly,
But we don't know why.
Maybe he was moving towards his prey,
A predator that should be locked up in --

Prisoners of our minds, children are.
I remember. I remember. I remember.
My mind knew that monsters live nearby,
My mind knew; it grew my own monsters under the bed.
Because the real monsters lived in towns.
Also nearby. Also unsafe.
The end of the day. It's three o'clock,
Everyone goes home from school.
The kids remembering the monsters.
They will remember, they continue to remember.

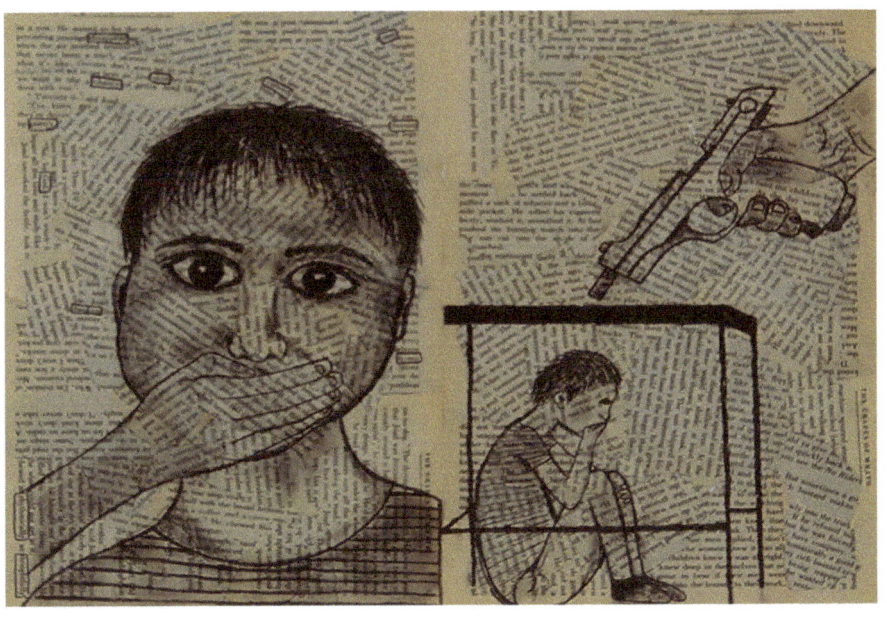

Gun

Ileana Viridiana Romero López

En Este Momento

Si tuviéramos todo el tiempo del mundo,
¿Qué te gustaría hacer?
Y si sólo tuviéramos hoy,
¿Cuál sería tu placer?
¿Te gusta esta vida?
¿Te gustó nacer?
¿De qué quieres platicar en este bonito amanecer?
Hay que apurarnos
Ya se va a oscurecer.

Ileana Viridiana Romero López

At This Moment

If we had all the time in the world,
What would you like to do?
And if we only had today,
What would your pleasure be?
Do you like this life?
Did you enjoy being born?
What do you want to talk about in this beautiful sunrise?
We must hurry
It is already getting dark.

Augustus Hoff

Elements

Look out the window, see the wind blow
See the grass shivering in the breeze
Red lights begin to flash
And bring man to their knees
What could it be?
Someone being the change they wished to see?
Or the buzzer beeping past it's snooze
Showing the world it's own views

Look out, the water is crashing
Moving and sifting the sand
Shields go up and the tears fall down
As the waves get what they planned
Is this what it's for?
Getting what's equal is asking for more?
Or turn the knob for your water
Waves crash out to come and slaughter

Look out, look out, the bullets rain
As the drops blow through the air
Don't look, if you don't care
Look out, take cover from the fire
Rake your leaves and roll up your sleeves

Because in this hell the only rule
Is what the man himself believes
Who did we choose?
Someone who litters the news?
Ignite the fire within you
To take out the man we knew

Look out, hide in the earth
Take refuge from the war
Words and lies take the show
Wait for combat or something more
Why does that control the door?
Opened or closed what's it all for?
It's just a game of cards
Leave the children with the guards

Storks

Katherine Kallas

The Worst Generation

How can you say that we are the worst generation?
Look in the mirror, you're the ones that raised us.
You say we are self-centered, I mean what did you expect?
You handed us iPads instead of teaching us self-respect.

You say we care too much about Instagram likes,
    but in the plastic age, validation is hard to come by.

Don't you see?
Parenting doesn't come from a TV.
Yet you sat us in front of it, a babysitter for free.

Your surprised when your baby girl is sexualized.
Your confused when your little boy doesn't treat women right.
Your excuse is to ignore until the problems are too big, then you
wish you could go back and teach us the lessons way back then.

Back then, when our minds were impressionable.
Back then, before our mistakes were regrettable.
But instead, you say the new generation is too far gone.
But from an early age, we were all conned.

We were told that everything we say is valid.
We were given participation trophies and now winning doesn't matter.
We have so much to learn and so much to fix.
But the only question seemed to be, *What is your Kik?*

We played Xbox instead of learning from textbooks.
We posted selfies instead of forming friendships.
We watched movies instead of playing outside.
Now in this society, all we do is hide.

Somya Wadhwa

Kill Your Darlings

Poem: Somewhere along the way of scrutiny and time,
    I have been taught how to despise myself.
Look pretty, darling, so that you can belong to someone
    someday
Because that's what a woman really wants, right?
Oh, sweetheart, look pretty but don't feel pretty
Meet your skin and bones, hair and face with conceited egoistic
    chorus
Sweetheart, self-solicitude is a sin
Knowing how to wear joy is nugatory if your body cannot
    wear that dress
Darling, you're the type of woman people don't look at
But they will stare at you if you don't follow their established
    echoic narcissistic accusations
You should mistake eyes for hands
Darling, why is your skin darker than an 'ideal' for a woman
Why are your hair shorter than your dignity
Why are your thighs fatter than your brain
Darling, why are you, you
Darling, you are made up of metaphors.
Darling, why is there a face on your pimples, don't let hormones
    fingerprint your face. But don't worry we'll get it all fixed
You haven't seen the actual you in years but, darling,
    It's not about you.

Sweetheart put on some lipstick. But not that red one,
　　it's too pretty for you
Put on some perfume. But not a strong one, you don't want to
　　attract attention
Put on some eyeshadow. But not that bright one, doesn't suit your
　　skin tone
Darling, change this physicality and, oh, that one, too
But don't you dare show yourself. You don't want to insinuate
　　the term beautiful in regards to a victim or a snack or a woman.
Darling, how old will you have to be to realize you need a 40+ skin
　　miracle cream and not a 30+
How old will you be till you look like a skeleton who pulled on
　　some skin
How old will you be till you realize being a woman does not
　　make you a man to be seen like a man is, you are a woman.
Because we are taught to live in a world where media pulls us out
　　from the womb and teaches us our first words
Fair and lovely, Fair and handsome
Darling, you are not a constant, you're a variable
But, darling, you are not looking for a casket of fortune
You don't look for a diet to slim your passion down
You don't look for a mirror to examine your dreams
Darling, you're a thought, an idea, a proposition, an abstraction.
Or maybe that's what everyone else is looking for.

Skeleton

Chloe Jane Rosenstock

Thanksgiving

I made an oath. My blood under mommy's fingernails
I never wear the bandages. She says I'll get infected, infested.
And I tell her I'm not afraid to die anymore. Mommy doesn't
  know how to detect my lies

Yesterday we went to the doctor to heal my broken bones
We fought like two children who don't yet know what it is to burn
I've decided ignorance is not bliss, For when mommy throws
  the daggers
She doesn't know where they land. But I do.

Oh, don't grab me so hard,
Your fingers leave breadcrumbs around my arms; I trace them
  back to you

Don't slam the door so loud, it echoes through these cardboard
  walls in our house you call home
And the back of your hand feels hot against my cheek, Mommy.

Have I said too much?
I wasn't bred in honesty. I breathe in the air of secrecy,
  drink it like milk!
But mommy doesn't like when I break diet, so keep it
  between us.

I made an oath. My blood under mommy's fingernails
I never wear the bandages—she says it's my own fault,
   all the biting,
So I decided I'd let silence fight my battles for me

Mommy fills in the gaps for both of us

Joss Aiken

Manipulate

You took your fingertips and smeared Lie on my head.

Lying on the ground, prickly edges of ivy leaves in my ear.
So close to the outside world.
Simple black metal of a schoolyard is what
Separated me from freedom, tied me to you.

But you took your voice and screamed Wrong in my ear.

Everything was a chess-game for you, me one pawn,
	you both armies.
If I had run away from you, what would you
Do? Would you crawl and creep over to me with your
	scrawled curses,
Would you whisper
Cyanide-sweet pollen into my garden of a head?
Yes, you would do all of it.

And you molded little soldiers to play with you,
	against Bitch me.

What oddities of mine irked you?
Where did my eccentricities push you over the edge?
Did they? Or did you enter a game,
Press Start, and then Shoot?

You unplugged my lifeline and plugged in your poison.
You taught everyone to think like you, even Dumb me.

Was I ever seen as little to you?
Or was my heart so big, you hated it?
Was my chest too large to ignore?
Or was my mind too unstoppable?
I am much more than you perceived,
Bigger than your small little set of values, vices,
    virtues, venoms.

I tasted your bite to kill and I survived.

Shivani Deshmukh

I Am a Women

I am the one
You will never get to know
I have scars, scars of my own
Scars that make me beautiful.

Some say, my smile is pretty,
Others tell me that I am icky.
Society forced me to notice,
My imperfections— as they call them
But this same society failed to realise
That these imperfections are my identity
I love them every angle

They say I will remain gullible
But these imperfections,
Are something that make me *Me*

They say, beauty is face
I say beauty is happiness
Happiness is not the absence of problems
It's the ability to deal with them

Yes, I was stronger
As my merriment descended
They were happy, contended
Because of my dreams and desires
They bring me down
They get happy when I drown

But I promise, I promise
This queen will rise to fight back
I am a women
Strong I was born to be
Victory was and still is in my blood
I will leave you wonderstruck

I am who I am,
A tigress by birth
I neither play victim nor do I point fingers
I stand and fight and rise
I am a women
And not who you want me to be
I am me.

Stippling Face

Sidra Nizami

I Am a Firework

Taken down by a single blow
I knew I was a loser, still they didn't let me go.

I guess, I forgot I had a choice
that I could stand up and raise my voice.

They thought they had me down,
that I won't stand my ground.

But what they did not see —
was, I had the flame ignited in me.

My knees are weak, my spine is broken
Yet, my soul is still alive and awoken.

It is high time, to show my worth,
Honey, I am a firework.

Sophia Gotham

Fly On

Dry skin, big brows, not small stomach.
Flaws?
Imperfections?
Or proof of uniqueness...?

Bad at relaxing, my science grade is the
Worst.
Failure?
Already?
Success can't happen overnight.

Baseball isn't my jam,
My hair is thin.
The imperfections we have aren't bad,
Our beauty isn't either.

Nothing is as it seems,
Everyone has dreams.
If someone tries to tell you who you are,
Who
You
Can
Be,
Keep your head up
And just
Fly on.

Elianna Lee

seven words of advice to a conflicted friend

love
is the seed
of everything good.

William Graham

Moonlight Man

There he stands,
Alone,
In the shallow part of the ocean.
The moonlight,
A natural spotlight,
Shines upon him as if he's part of the earth itself.
He watches the horizon as if he's waiting for something to show,
But nothing ever appears.
The shallow waves tackle his ankles,
Ever so gently,
Attacking him in the smoothest way.
I watch from behind,
Amazed in a unkindled awe,
At his serenity.
His peace...it's beautiful.
Then,
In the reveried horizon,
A wave has started.
I watch as it starts off as a child's plaything,
Into a monstrous beast running across the water.
Fear pokes at my chest,
As if needles are being pulled from inside me by a magnet,
But he still stands there.

Watching,
Calmly,
As the monstrosity comes for him.
Is this death coming in another form?
I try to scream,
To warn him to move...to run,
But no words manifest and I myself is unable to move.
Stuck in a tight hold by this moist sand.
The beast runs towards him,
Increasing it's pace,
Ready to sweep him away.
Then,
Slowly,
He turns around.
His eyes,
Turquoise pearls,
Look at mine connecting more than just mere eyesight.
Pain twists in my chest because the supposed Moonlight
 Man is me and I,him.
He opens his mouth and the wind carries his voice to my ear.
It's ok
As I hear his last word,
The beast consumes him...leaving not a trace behind.
This unknown pain feels eternal,
It feels as if it will never fade away.
The sand lets go of its invisible death grip on my legs as I move
 towards the spot, where *I* once stood.

I look at the horizon,

Its beauty,

Puts me in a unwavering trance.

A trance that milks away the pain,

That gives me peace,

And that makes it all actually feel ok.

As I continue watching,

I see a small wave and unbelievably, it's more beautiful than anything i've ever seen.

Beach

Katherine Kallas

Beauty is Pain

Beauty is pain.
She whispers the words under her breath as she sucks in her stomach, tightening her corset.
She damages her skeletal structure for the night; squishing her organs like jello.
Who needs organs anyway?
A small price to pay for the hourglass shape.

Beauty is pain.
She thinks as she shoves her feet into her heels.
Gritting her teeth as she walks.
But they make her legs look so good.
Because everyone can see her legs in the darkness of the night.
In her mind, people will whisper.
Whisper about the girl that wore flats - how dare she!

Beauty is pain.
She says as she burns her ear on a curling iron.
It does not hurt as much as it used to.
She has gotten accustomed to the throbbing.
Numb to the brand of the iron mark that shows she has a social life.
That she has a reason to doll herself up.
Proof that she has the ability to be pretty, as long as she has the proper tools.

Beauty is pain.
She tells herself as needles poke her lips, filling them into the desired plump shape.
Subconsciously, she still feels like the ugly girl who was made fun of in middle school.
If they could only see her now they might think she's cool.

Beauty is pain.
Skin wrinkled from pulling, and blending, and shading, and the painting she did with her makeup brush.
The Picasso of her painting, she is so used to manipulating, she doesn't recognize the girl in the mirror.
Picasso, more like Houdini, the illusion of beauty.
The best magic trick ever achieved.

Beauty is pain.
As she breathes into a tube.
Going under.
One last final procedure.
She tells herself, *After this, I'll be perfect.*
After this, I'll be worth it.
After this, it will all be worth it.
After all, beauty is pain.

Narine Verdiyan

Fell in Love with Lonely
-after muni

lonely comes and visits me when the lights are off
she wasn't invited, but it's an unspoken pact we both made that
she comes, i sit with her
she's keeps me company

lonely and i talk about our day, how it failed us
how our day promises the next one will be better
so we believe it
sleep, 24 hours
deja vu is funny in the sense
of being met with the same disappointment

i run a bath for the both of us, i let her sit behind me and
    wash my hair
she massages the back of my neck to unwind tension,
    but it is almost as if she is the one tying the knots
we sit in the bath until the water begins to boil
until the feeling of guilt melts off along with our skin

we almost have too much in common
the way we lick our lips after eating black holes
we have fear in common
gnawed into our bones

i ask her to stay another night, we're both scared
she says yes
she cuddles me cold that night

i fall in love with her bit by bit
she must notice
her grip gets tighter in my hands as i dont leave bed
doesn't question when i eat my 7th frozen waffle that day
i get phone calls but i leave them when lonely is glowing
    with beauty
when lonely shows me that the dark holds its own light

lonely's caught me now
and i'm afraid it's much too late
to leave

Dream

Minerva Macarrulla

I Tell Everyone Who Asks That the Reason My Phone Is Entirely in Spanish Is Because It Helps Me Learn Faster; Closer to the Truth Is That It Helps Me Remember

My father learned Spanish twice—
Once, skipping across banter entrenched in a sunbeam no
    sunscreen hot enough to
thaw baby teeth into vowel sounds as elongated as a stalk of
    his grandmother's
sugarcane and R's set on rolling as undulantly as the hills in
    La Vega my father learned
Spanish from the bursting paints of the walls of the Colonial
    District and the Jesuits in
Santo Cerro and the second time my father learned Spanish

he skipped across written narrative entrenched in homogenous
American English TV and the aftermath of wanting to belong
    cold enough
to freeze teenage teeth into stillness my father remembered
    Spanish
because of the bursting paints he brought to his canvases
memory retreating to a carnival fantasy reminding him of
    the magic it was

to undulate with the hills of La Vega, R's that won't stop rolling
and vowels that won't stop elongating
and comradery with the banter, the sunbeam,
the sugar cane and the Jesuits in Santo Cerro. I imagine him:
novel in one hand, Spanish-English dictionary in
the other, reconstructing the language
that would never again become quite automatic enough to him
to pass it seamlessly
from his lips to my own.
The day he opened his mouth to speak
on the phone across the ocean again, Dolores said it must have
    been someone else.
Sé que Manuel ya no habla el español.

My father still speaks Spanish like a native speaker,
but you would never guess from his accent that it was
Dominican banter
Caribbean sun
abuela's sugarcane and the Jesuits in Santo Cerro
that taught him to speak
the first time.

My father learned Spanish twice
and I am trying my best to just remember
the first time.

Nataly Kazzi

Like the Sky Holds Its Shining Stars

I.
Dear body;
You are my home

And I should have loved you more; should have been
    stronger for you.
Instead of throwing you in the palm of his hands
Believing his beautiful words that i couldn't resist.

He used you
like you are just made of flesh and bones
He broke your golden heart into a million fragments

I should have embraced your scars
That hold endless stories
like the sky holds its shining stars

II.

I was the perfect child, innocent
I believed that life was a fairytale
Until I learned that not every story ends with a happy ending
Nobody told me not to trust a man
before a night partying with my friends

I knew they didn't believe me when I returned home,
tears racing down my cheeks,
Dress stained with my dead stars

they blamed me for having a nice body,
wearing that dress i bought for myself and not to impress anyone
they blamed me for being a woman… but who blamed him?

Now a simple touch of my hand can trigger a memory..
they don't understand how
my body has become a haunted house

remembering his breath on my neck,
the smell of alcohol and cigarettes,
the sound of my dress unzipping

he became a ghost under my bed
a shadow that follows me everyday
Everytime i try to close my eyes
I see myself trapped like bug
on a spiders web, unable to move,
he owned the body I called mine.

III.
men think we exist for them
They treat our bodies like a buffet
taking what they want
Over and over again.

But i am not just made of flesh and bones
I cry and feel pain
I can learn self-defense
I can earn a six-figure salary.
I can fight in the military, give birth, run marathons and run for president.

I stand with survivors to provide resources for gender based violence
I stand with survivors in the DRC that are demanding justice,
like Anna Maria Archila and Maria Gallagher,
the two sexual assault survivors who confronted politician jeff flake
While he was on his way to cast his vote for Brett Kavanaugh.

They remind us that our voices are powerful

I stand with myself
I am a strong, deliberate, confident, loving woman
I will let no man
take that away from me

IV.
this time I am smiling at my body,
the body I hated for so long
because my love for him was bigger
than the love I share with myself

But look at me now
my self love opened of the cage
I am finally free from the fear was feeding on my confidence like a hungry beast.

my body is a constellation full of shining diamonds
you can call it whatever u want
But this body,
This work of art…

I will call it mine

I am a woman
And I know my voice will change everything

Ashley Kim

Foreign Tongues

Diversity is a curse.
And failure to revel in the opaque vowels of the lettered
  white-man
is a sin worthy of excommunication.
Why introduce knotted tongues to the purity of a neatly-woven
  America?

I have assiduously re-programmed myself
to regard my tongue as nothing less than *American*—
prideful of having sloughed my tongue of its Asian snake-skin,
no longer labeled as a *migrant* worth shunning
by the clunky inflections that arrest her foreign tongue.

Yet my mother sits at her vanity with a glass of wine,
laboriously mouthing an ill-fitting language in the mirror,
her tongue clumsily dancing a tango, not knowing that America
is a waltz.

And though my mother's American label reads *alien, intruder,*
  displaced,
I feel my own tongue paralyzed by an unexpected shame,
for despite my efforts I have found,
that as unnatural and alien as is my mother's tongue,
that in escaping the foreigner's label,
I am a different kind of refugee,
One adrift from her own identity.

Music

Jasmine Li

System Error: Shutdown Imminent

These pretty girls will smile,
Say everything is fine.

You will believe them
You will watch as
bone turn to dust
Skin turns to paper
Smiles to frowns
Covered by a thick layer of bullshit and lipstick
They are fine, 100% fine.

But they are asking, begging, pleading for help.
And everyone ignores the signs.
You will watch them waste away
But by the time you realize
There will be no one left to save

Because girls are objects
Meant to be used
Meant to be sexy
So when sexy turns to sick
and sobbing on the bathroom floor
And ribs cave in from hunger's tough

Smiles fade
Rosy cheeks rosy no more

Throw them away
after all, girls are fundamentally flawed, fragile, fallible
replaceable
each model better than the next
Alpha, beta, 1.0, 2.0

New update available
Would you like to upgrade
Y/N?

Ok, update initializing.

Download failed.
Would you like to try again?

Bhagyashree Barman

The World's Waking up

Seeing those hopeless eyes
Hearing those remorseful cries
I begged lord to stop

We pray good for us
Did we ever just looked at the outside world
Next time you travelling make sure you have the windows
    down in the bus

To see the social evils
Not only poverty
The children working at the mills

Life could be tough sometimes
Some people don't want to be
The main character of their own lives

We see gender inequality
We see mob lynching
Helpless prisoners of war

The rich gets richer
The poor gets poorer
Do innocent people always have to suffer?

With the coming of Democracy
Paving it's way in different countries
A hope of joy ecstasy

Democracy doing it's job
Social justice is what we wanted
So that there are less sobs

New generation, the old and the conservatives
Injustice might be more powerful
But in the end justice triumphs
As the world is waking up.

Hands

Rayna Bowman

See Me

I see you
It's time you see me
The other you've let replace me
Does not want you to see me
Why do you hide me
What have they lead you to believe
What they say is not the truth you see
They say sticks and stones may break my bones
But words will never hurt me.
But don't you see
Their words broke me
These words they claim won't hurt me
Are the exact reason i'm unworthy
For the public eye to see
I'm tucked away like the sun on a cloudy day
Trying to shine
Reclaim what was once mine
You think i'm covered completely
But i find ways to shine briefly
The clouds threw the day
Quickly turns gray
Then when she drained
Here comes the rain
Then it floods

She's thinking of turning to drugs
I've surfaced
This is not a good thing that means she's feeling worthless
This is only time i truly shine
here to pick up the pieces the other left behind
I try to convince her
she need me nothing else will fix her
Something's different this time
This time i will shine
I'm not going away
It's me the real you that will stay
And the other is banished to the clouds
To stay and drown
I'm back i hope you feel less pain
Because i am the real you i've erased the stain
No more being what other want for there attain
You're now truly you again
I've seen you
Now you see me

Ava Minu-Sepehr

Nastaran (the Love Song)

Iranian music makes me feel sick.
The way death draws air from the parts of your body
you did not know breathed.
I am fully aching, in the moment
my grandma lifts me in her arms
plays Iranian music from the Iranian radio station
moves her hands this way
this way
that way
the curl so graceful

the curve of the music so suddenly wakes me
in her absence, in the loss of everything I clung to.
The music pulls everything I don't own but
want to own
from my stomach
the moment in the market and there's these words
they are no different than other words
why must we travel so many miles for these,
still flung so far from their home.

Everything I am missing still exists
the Iranian music reminds me
I am just here

what is time
when the words are so folded and comforting.
I turn off the radio because it's gone,
you're gone
a blaze of red slowly bleeds out along this white.

The fruit bowl in the living room is no longer full
and no one realizes the catastrophe
the couch is pushed back and the stains
there the Iranian music still plays from the Iranian radio
    station
as if to remind me
I'm still here and you're still
gone, so lost in the way the music makes me feel gutted

strew out along the ground
my words
I am too small to pick them up.

Katherine Kallas

Drugged Dream

Her pen is a needle as she scribbles on her skin.
She is writing a make-believe story in which she is the heroine.
But she is not brave now, her captor is heroin.

Relapse is the contract she signed long ago.
She knows all too well the red and blue glows.

In her story, she is the knight in shining armor.
But in her neurotic state, reality could not be any farther.

Chalk outline on the sidewalk.
The same ice that froze her clock.
The castle on the hill is a mere dream that she has long forgot.

Crystals are just pretty pistols.
Bullets and shattered glass.
Didn't know how much was too much because she had already
    turned to ash.

White cross on a suburban lawn.
Spread out through the city.
American dream.
But Christy and Amy took the liberty.

She is married now, the bottle is her husband.
A wedding band on her hand, in the other, her substance.

R'keria Davis

Possession of a Smell

prancing around you,
my lime green eyes scrape
the eucalyptus scent
off your legs.

i enter,
invading your holiness,
angel voices slapping the ground
and smoke mingling
with your soft, chestnut hair.

gasoline drips
from your nostrils,
coloring my skin.

menthol treads along your nose hairs,
rises like cooled water,
and crystalizes.

we dance with new smells.

a nicotine covered
beginning you are for me,
another set of skin cells.

Rayna Bowman

Envy

Why must you make me
Why must you use me
Why must you ruin me
Envy is the name you bare
or at least the one you choose to share
when doing your undercover work
oh how it makes me hurt.
You started with my leaves
ruining the beautiful part of me
Next you burn my roots
that's what you do
make sure i cannot regrow
the parts of me that define me so
but i refuse to believe
in the power you hold over me
i refuse to believe
you're what's destroying me
I cannot be the only one who knows
the real name you hold
so i'll be sure to let everyone know
how the bond we once shared has broke
leave me alone
or i'll expose the real name you hold

the name that brings chills to my bones
so i beg and plead
that you give me room to breath
give me room to eradicate the dirty seed
you planted in place of my tree
i beg and plead
leave me be
Jealousy

Dominique Cuningkin

Individualism

We're free but constantly told how to live life
Go to school, get good grades, be active, and play nice
Obey authority and rules and life will be just fine
Even though your circumstances may be different from mine

For every different math problem, use different equations
Shouldn't we apply that to every situation?
Because while I just may be able to commit facts to memory
Someone else has to learn by actually doing

But since she can't sit still and moves too much
They give her a new label and prescription drugs
You see the withdrawal written all of her face
She feels that she's dumb but that's not even the case

Let us be independent, let us be free
Stop trying to make your issues apply to me
Stop putting meat on a vegetarian's plate
I live my own life, and make my own mistakes

Molly Duke

Grab Her

Subject A has been on the earth for sixteen years.
And through those sixteen years she has begun to understand
    why so many students crave a beer instead of a soda or a
    lemonade.
Because when a man is told to grab her by the pussy, a beer is
Synonymous to a year.
Synonymous to the amount of time that a beer can make
    disappear.
The time that was once one for happiness, filled with friends
    and nights out.
Now she sits at home
On a couch
And sips on a beer that
Is as warm as her tears.

On year fourteen of sixteen she sees the sneers.
The sneers of her classmates that call her easy, call her a slut, c
    all her a down right whore for the next two years;
Because a man thought grabbing a pussy would be greeted with
    cheers
Only to be told that no they were tears and not cheers because
Fuck man that's messed up and the ridicule is
foreign as he volunteers to repeat it, to do it one more time

Because baby he promises to make her feel good
And her tears are suddenly synonymous to those years spent
　on the couch.

Those years that fly by as she learns to cross her legs to avoid the
　jeers
As she learns to cover her body so she draws no attention to herself.
As she learns that her body is not viewed as her own.
As she learns that no matter what, she was asking for it.
As she learns those jeers are supposed to be taken as a compliment.
The jeers of the men in bars who offer her a beer to throw away
　the years.
Who would think she would drink away her fears as they veer to
　alcoholism
Instead of going to therapy
Or going to support
Because a beer only costs three dollars while help is hundreds
and five years had passed in those beers because a man was told
To grab her by the pussy.

Katherine Kallas

Grim Reaper in the High School

A depressed teen is like a paper clip.
On a stack of papers, trying to hold it together, try not to rip.
Until it breaks and the words spill out onto the floor.
Full of unanswered questions like, what's all this for?

A depressed teen is a whisper through cracked lips,
    out of a dry throat.
Or a piece of burnt toast, too common these days.
Locker hook missing a coat.
A choir missing a note.
A half-finished coke.

A depressed teen is the girl who sits silently in the classroom.
A depressed teen is that one blonde chick who always wears
    too much perfume.
A depressed teen is the captain of the football team.
The class clown, or the drama queen.

The depressed teen smiles.
Or doesn't.
But the depressed teen tries to not show they are depressed.
Try to hide it.
Disguise it.

Dress it up to cover the cuts on their wrists.
Scars covered by missing assignments.
Depression is a high school's terrorist.

Unnoticed.

Until gunshots ring out, bullets hitting metal lockers.
Until screams flow out of the fountains instead of water.
Until blood is the ink in the knives they use to write their essays.
Until the suicide rate is higher than grades.
Until all of us are left guessing, what happened to them anyway?

In the cafeteria bones of their classmates are served on plastic trays.
Babies dying in the ninth grade.
The janitor now mops up brains from the hallways.
Students cry instead of going to ball games.

Health class students dissecting organs from members of their own class.
Because they are better than a bag of dead rats.
More common than in the past.

Textbooks full of obituaries, of all the lives lost since January.
Names blur together, easily forgotten.
While their ghosts don't come back to school next autumn.

Because they don't get a summer break.
They linger in the science lab trying to find that assignment they misplaced.

They are the messages carved into the bathroom walls.
They mixed up the experiment and their lives they dissolved.
In a beaker.
The next day during roll call the name without a speaker.
Grim Reaper in the high school.

Rehma Khan

The Impervious Hue of Hope

What makes a bird re-live
the moments of scorching heat,
when even the dawn durst not spread its wings
in a land oh so bleak
Audacious enough to believe,
where never hope had been harbored,
that soon it shall outlive their deceits
in their very own empire.
Clogged, whipped and artfully bereaved
of the freedom with which the bird once used to breathe
The wounds did, after all, heal
but the emancipation never got retrieved.
Hard enough to live it once;
impossible to re-live the agony all over again.
By entrapping the innocent betwixt the tendrils,
they can seize not its power to hope.
Clasp it tighter!
It might elope,
they cry entrapping it in the fetters anew.
What makes them think that they can imbue
the bird in their own hues?
It is but their unbecoming ignorance.
Uprooted is the scent of the fragrance

that once pervaded their kingdom
Brutality now has become
their sole emblem.

Look now not back
in the direction of the hamlet,
where dwells your flock
The bird consoles whilst soliloquizing,
Have not I endured
their insults, as I, they mocked?
They think me blind,
but their cruelty, I see
They think me dumb,
Unaware of the urges
my heart whispers with each beat
Fire and darkness,
in every maneuver of theirs have I seen
But come a day, there shall
when the sun will rise again
by the integrity of my conviction
and to live wholly this day, indeed,
do I re-live each time
these moments of scorching heat.

Migration

Rialin Yasay

The Drought

Breaking rocks of fairness; cracking ground of felicity;
Wilting and dying flowers of peace and serenity;
Weakening trees of people's freedom, and drying rivers of solidarity —
The mournful happenings in the society that has a drought of justice and equality.

A prestigious place for the nobles and dry ground for the peasants —
The scorned that have been treated and seen as sulky, and full of predicaments —
Have brought the chaos and conflict which consisted this calamity:
The drought that we never dreamt of, and has become a nightmare reality.

The extreme temperature of graft and corruption in diverse adverse ways;
The burning sun of greed that encroaches the rights of others through its rays;
And the enormous hot gases of oppression in the atmosphere —
The detrimental events which have caused this drought to appear.

This calamity has made us, the people whose eyes are wide open,
Pour the clouds of our hearts with hate, sorrow, and distress.

As the drought in the society, which is separated by social classes,
Becomes worse, the clouds of our hearts become heavier.

Despite that, we have never let our voices and actions—
 in the form of rain —
Pour out of the clouds of our hearts, and our pain to drain,
Because of the thought that it won't stop the drought
No matter how loud and bountiful the rain would shout.

However, we haven't realized that every single drop of rain —
A single voice and action that has been wanting for peace to rise again,
And has been waiting for the time to be heard, and be thought about —
Is powerful and has the potential to change the fate of the drastic drought.

We should fight this calamity by pouring out our voices and actions.
Let these speak the truth, and create change to attain our satisfaction.
Let us not let the drought of justice and equality reign,
But let's help each other to regenerate our society by the powerful rain.

Let us reform the rocks of fairness, nourish the ground of felicity,
Bloom with the flowers of peace and serenity,
Strengthen the people's freedom, and abound the rivers of solidarity,
In order to revitalize our society and cease the drought of justice and equality.

Water Crisis

Ava Minu-Sepehr

I Can't Go There Now

I dreamed
I reached Iran.

I reached Iran wearing a chador
but it's loose and kind.
The street unfolds, the cars
flood streets grey.

I reached Iran and am standing on the sidewalk.
The other two are pleasantly
behind me.
Isn't everything like that here.

(I reached Iran)
(and everything is behind us)
(I am like everyone)
(my name)
(just simply unconditionally)
(I am enough of me)
(a full stomach)
(a deep ache)

Sunlight leaks in.
I reached Iran pure and filtered in soft light.

I held something,
I remember
dropping it
my dress.

I reached Iran with
no shoes on
my feet.

I reached Iran
and my knees brushed the ground,
collapsed on the pavement.
Blurred light life.
I heard people in my tongue
mouths so warm I could weep--
sit in them and build my home.
Thick words like cheeks full of
sugar cubes.
I have fallen with my hands over my head.
I give myself up
gently
to cry.

I reached Iran.
Could I reach you and I did.
I know you.

I reached Iran and kissed the earth.

Taylor Drummer

Drugs Money Women

What's a young nigga to do?
Stuck in this shit hole
You give em'
Drugs, Money, Women
And expect him not to use

Condemned to grow ignorant
Malnourished of resources
Raised in poverty
And scarcity of authentic guidance
What do you think will happen?

No prevalent black leaders present
They end up killed
I ruminate why
That's what this country loves and fears most:
a minority with knowledge
The only way to stop him is to off him

Trying our best to suffice
With the cards we were dealt
Life is hard so we cope with
Drugs Money Women
It's a brief escape from this fucked up world

I don't blame em'

Drizzle Bayer

Quiet Your Mind

I can't write down any words, for I have nothing worthwhile to say
I'm watching through screens as I say what I don't mean,
I'm outdated tech, I can't function right.

What can I say, what can I do, it's never the way I think, or hope
You perceive me in a way that I am not because
My mind won't allow itself to be seen, and you can't find me
You don't even know what to look for, and I can't tell you
I don't know either, so all I can do is stay lost, wandering,
Looking through the bars of the cage I built around myself,
With no entrance or exit

Just silence as I sit there with the incomprehensive thoughts
    in my head
With no way in and no way out.

Shhh... the voices say. *Quiet your mind.*

But how can I quiet my mind when all I want to do is scream
    the words
That get stuck in my throat and are instead labelled as stammers?
I have no outlet so I have to think because there is no quiet
    and there is no end.

I'm stuck in a loop and I can't get out,
I'm trying to speak but all they can tell me is to

Shhh... quiet your mind.

I'm supposed to stay silent and push away the thoughts that have been banging
On the walls of my mind with no avail for so, so long.
I'm supposed to give up and give in and throw all the fighting away?
I will never get to say anything worthwhile, because the best advice I ever got was just

Shhh... quiet your mind.

And I listened.

And because I shushed my mind, I gave leeway to
My already broken vocal cords to rust. Placed on a shelf, never to be used again,
Forever collecting dust.
My voice will never be used to say anything worthwhile.
It ran out of fight.

Because what's the use in a voice fighting for the chance to be heard,
If there is nothing but a quiet mind behind it?

Distorted Reality

Mion Charity

Beauty Lies

beautiful yet mysterious
she lies upon a bed
waiting to be shown
how to handle the beauty and all it depicts
will they reveal?
or merely repent
the avant garde temple that is her
yet they set to disappoint
they will not tell her
let her have such power
a myriad of lies
but dutifully so
she withers away
given no truth
or will
ending the suffering
to escape
the city of lies.

Rayna Bowman

Revelation

They teach us to…
fear rejection,
crave affection,
and dream of perfection,
But there is no real correction,
For this lost of direction,
We can't explain this corruption,
We see in are reflection,
We need a eruption,
Of total redemption,
Or we'll never find are way out of this hole
We fail to mention
So we need hold a convention,
To find a solution,
Because this dysfunction is infusing confusion,
And we realize this is nothing but an illusion,
Now we're left to fight infection,
So they can pick out a section,
To add to their collection,
But if we find are way around this deception,
And let are commotion be found in are devotion,
To stop this erosion,
Of our emotion,
We'll be free of this contraption,
That wields our actions,
And leaves us for extraction

Minerva Macarrulla

Thawing

every time I have stepped outside in the past two months
I have thought of the word *thaw*
its jagged fade to violence, the smooth edge of its blade
…slick in the underbrush
its softness an alibi for slow suffocation
the way it makes home at our extremes …hides outside of our range
releases permafrost from its misery
releases the wall of a greenhouse to choke our stars
the way it makes home too at the December air in Brooklyn
subtler there and still more here… tonight I landed in San Diego
the drive away from the airport cradled me,
the air was kind to my skin… I had to wonder
if this was not just a prank on a thawing New York if I, lucid
from plane seat and greenhouse concern, had imagined the journey
and still stood in the same air… not cradling and kind like I thought
just a fading edge slick in the suffocation
jaggedly smooth in the underbrush, slow… and thawing

Dana Abou-Diab

Pride!

This piece of fabric
I can wear it with pride
But the world keeps reminding me.
The pride slips as fast as the words from the mouths
What does this scarf mean?
I wear it on my head like a symbol of my faith
But the meaning is twisted
The danger increases
Violence is heard and seen all around!
A simple walk on the street can trigger a thought
Like the shot of a gun!
This hijab can show who I am
And reveal the thoughts...
What is the price of this symbol? My life?

Like a bullet through a wall
The words are shot through the world
The words hurt even when they don't truly reach me
I see the eyes that stare
The curiosity of others
Is she dangerous?
Isn't that unfair?
The scarf was a choice
A choice that should be held with pride
NOT fear!

Every night, I can walk
But the eyes that watch think me a target
Or more, a target to me

This scarf shows who I am
But no one else can see that!
Pride or Fear? How should I wear it?
I can walk out, tall and strong-
But with the risk of being hurt by another
Whether a gun or gossip—sure I can ignore
But one person can tell more and more until-
More bad views… and those damage pride
And then the rocks just keep hitting the glass

I'm not dangerous! I want to yell, *I won't hurt you!*
But they wouldn't listen if I did
I am just a small voice among the many of the popular

If a person dresses the same way as another
Does that mean they are both the same?
If I go out with a weapon to kill—
does that mean everyone who wears this same fabric—
is no different?

Fear- or Pride? Will it even matter…
NO! Pride!
Show people nothing is worth the fear!
Show them NOT to run!

Hijab and Hair

Elizabeth Bowling

Humiliation

Note to the American Republic
Step One of becoming the greatest nation on Earth
Make them dependent on us
Spread the word that
We the people are a nation of equality
Of liberty
And justice
For all
Give us your tired
Your poor
Your huddled masses yearning to breathe free
And we will make them our servants
We will make them our scapegoats
We will make them work for pennies
From coast to coast
Let them do the dirty work
We don't want to do!
Let their name be
People who will take jobs no one else will
Because we have moved past these dirty low-class jobs
And then we will complain about them
We will say they are taking all our jobs
We will erase the words carved in our history
Erase our very blood

We will blame them for all our problems
We will take away their children
We will make them the enemy suspected and hunted
And we will build a wall
To keep our past away
Humiliation
What tool is there stronger
Save Hunger
And Fear
Its brothers and sisters
We will worry about our clothes
And forget where we got them
While they break backs
And take hard jobs
And do whatever they must
So that they too might partake in America
There are many places to finish college late
But where to go to learn English?
We scoff at the fact that we might learn their language
And instead we'll laugh at their attempts
To speak our immigrant language
Because our language is better
Our customs are better
Our traditions are better
Humiliation
The trade of America

Elephant

Elizabeth Bowling

If I Ever . . .

If I Ever
Said Mother, laughing,
Spend thousands on a piece of clothing
Slap me
We laughed together then
Thinking how ridiculous it was
That someone would pay so much for what they got
Now I am laughing for a different reason
At another world
Another situation
Where someone refused to pay themselves
And is searching for another wallet
I am told to
Never disobey
Curse words are forbidden
And so are slurs
Treat everyone equally
And be responsible
And If I Ever did wrong . . .
But this nation is so blind
If I Evers
Have been done countless times
If I Ever

Read a book too adult
I'd get in trouble
If I Ever
Said I was weird
I'd get a lecture
But if they ever
Separate families
That's just politics
And there is nothing wrong
Were I to become a slut
All would turn against me
But look at what we're doing
Lying with the sluts of the world
And
Everyone
Thinks it's okay
Or at least they see nothing wrong
I stare at the television screen
Longing to speak out
Yet frightened to
If I ever . . .

Child Labor

Katie Vandermel

The Gay Rose

There's a label to everything: The
'Organic'-ness of your whole grain bread, a precursor
to its worth in your belly. Or
The letters living in the alphabet, like the 'B' on your psychology
    exam, a societal metric
of your intelligence. Or
The color of your skin, a creamy chocolate.
A shade bitter sweet, cocoa under-grown.

But hate can emanate from even more perilous spheres.
    It can wound
even those with the most incredible incandescence of spirit
your best friend.

The one running like a kite, singing deathless song.

Give him a belle
and he would make you a mirror.
Give him your roses
and he would give you a deity's embrace
Give him your tears and
he would lift you in the dark.

But he has a secret.
Two fingers to two lips.

He likes boys.

The earth would come whipping his backside if his parents
    knew because
there is a bad, bad, label for boys who like boys.

His song has grown quiet
A voice in the dark

Wilting roses, no longer gay.

Thayse Souza dos Santos Santos

Mundo Revirado

O mundo está ao contrário
Tudo está estranhamente mudado
Estamos com TODOS nossos direitos
Brutalmente desrespeitados
Direitos de anos atras
ignorados, mascarados!

É sempre a mesma notícia
Logo cedo, no mundo todo
Hoje mais um humano
Destruiu uma família,
Ceifou a vida do outro
Isso está virando um *costume* mundial
Está se transformando em algo natural.

Os direitos deveriam servir
A todos, não importa a quem
Mas infelizmente
Você é bem ou mal tratado
Dependendo do que você tem
Não há proteção a ninguém
Homens mulheres e crianças
Estão na lista também...

Vamos ter perseverança
Lutar com legitimidde
Não podemos deixar o preconceito invalidar
Os direitos da humanidade...

Thayse Souza dos Santos Santos

Upside Down World

The world is upside down
Everything strangely changed
ALL our rights are
Brutally disdained
Rights of years ago
ignored, masked!

It's always the same news
Early in the morning, all around the world
Today another human
Destroyed a family,
Reaped the life of others
This is becoming a worldwide norm.

Rights should serve
everyone, it does not matter who.
Unfortunately, you are well or poorly treated
depending on what you have.
There is no protection for anyone
Men, women and children, all the same…

Let's have perseverance
Fight with legitimacy
We cannot let prejudice invalidate
The rights of humanity...

Giselly Kamily de Jesus Santos Santos

Tempos Sombrios

Trazidos em um navio
Onde o chão era frio
Povo condenado, injustiçado!
Condenados para viver
Como míseros escravos...

Homens açoitados, forçados a trabalhar
Mulheres abusadas com seus bebês para carregar
Crianças magras e sem ninguém para amar
Será essa uma época, que queremos adorar?

Homens e mulheres sendo laçados ao mar
De dentro de um navio, sombrio!
Em seu mundo solitário e vazio.
Que vida cruel, meu BRASIL!!!

Os míseros escravos,
comiam a comida que o diabo amassava
Eram tratados como pássaros
Presos em suas jaulas desgraçadas
Naquele local, a dor permanecia
Sem nenhum respeito, com suas vidas vazias.

Mas, isso não acabou!
A sociedade hipócrita não deixou.
Seja gay, seja pobre, seja negro!
Ainda não temos, o tão clamado respeito.

Seja humanamente racional
O mundo merece respeito
E você, está deixando isso para o final
Respeite!!! Nossa história pode até te servir no final,
Como uma reflexiva lição de moral!!!

Giselly Kamily de Jesus Santos Santos

Dark Times

Brought on a ship
Where the ground was cold
People condemned, wronged!
Condemned to live
Like miserable slaves ...

Men whipped, forced to work
Abused women with their babies to carry
Children thin and without anyone to love
Is this a time we want to worship?

Men and women being laced to the sea
From inside a ship, grim!
In their lonely and empty world.
What a cruel life, my BRAZIL!!!

The miserable slaves,
they ate the food that the devil kneaded
They were treated like birds
Trapped in their wretched cages
At that place, the pain remained
Without any respect, with their emptied lives.

But this is not over!
The hypocritical society did not leave.
Be gay, be poor, be black!
We still have not the so-called respect.

Be humanly rational
The world deserves respect
And you, you're leaving it to the end.
Respect!!! Our story may even serve you in the end,
As a lesson for moral reflection!!!

Pablo Montalvão

Ritual Poético

Por favor, escreva seu poema nesse espaço: Ritual Poético
A poesia vislumbra, se iguala a vida e apronta
Ela apaga minhas dores, mas não paga minhas contas
E o eu lírico... o que diz? Tudo está por um triz
Ela julga e condena, sendo seu próprio juiz
Toda verdade d'baixo do nosso nariz
Eu não sabia! Pensei; toda vez que espirrasse fosse só alergia
E quanto vale a alegria? Consciência sem peso, dia após dia

Se a cada ritual poético
Possuir-vos pudesse, possuir-vos-ia

Meu artista interno oculto, uma salva de palmas!
Meu maior sentimento de luto, uma enxurrada de traumas
Após qualquer tempestade, há um momento de calma
A poesia não mata a fome, mas, alimenta a alma
Nem todo choro é por dor. Por tanta falta de amor
Para calcular tamanha angustia, não haverá contador
A sociedade se torna um tumor
E não haverá cirurgia

Se a cada ritual poético
Possuir-vos pudesse, possuir-vos-ia.

Pablo Montalvão

Poetic Ritual

Poetry gleams, equals life and is mischievous
It erases my pains, but it does not pay my bills
And the lyrical self ... what does it say? Everything is by a thread
It judges and condemns, being its own judge.
All truth under our nose
I did not know! I thought every time I sneezed it was just allergy.
And how much is joy worth? Consciousness without guilt, day after day.

If every poetic ritual
Could possess you, it would.

My hidden inner artist, a round of applause!
My biggest mourning, a flood of traumas
After every storm, there is a moment of calm
Poetry does not kill hunger, but it nourishes the soul.
Not every cry is of pain or lack of love.
To calculate the size of such anguish, no accountant will do
Society becomes a tumor
No surgery will do

If every poetic ritual
Could possess you, it would.

Random Collage

Michelle María Gómez Álvarez

Resistir lo Cotidiano

Resisten mis ojos retorcidos los gritos de mi madre
por la falta de dinero, la ausencia de mi padre,
habitante en el cuarto de trebejos del abuelo.
Mi padre, envuelto en su alcoholismo pendenciero.
Resisto estudiar física y química entre la narcomúsica
ensordecedora de vecinos drogados sin prejuicios.

Estudio entre la tierra de mi pueblo y el asfalto de la ciudad.
Me alimento de becas, ayuda de mis tíos y una actitud estoica
para tener a salvo el viejo nogal, la higuera, bugambilias,
geranios rosales y malvones que antaño cultivaron los abuelos.
Árboles y plantas me ayudan a respirar y evitar vicios
    tremebundos
en que caen jóvenes de mi edad y no regresan nunca.
Ayudo a la naturaleza con lo aprendido en la escuela y sociedad.

No fumaré nicotina, no beberé cerveza, ni whisky, ni tequila;
mucho menos sabré de adicciones sintéticas que matan
    a los pobres
y a los actores miserables de la televisión.

Estudio con estoicismo para ayudar a la naturaleza y a mi
    generación.

No seré presa de modas ni consumismo exorbitante.
Resistir con mucha fe, disciplina, estudio y sabia práctica, lo mismo en la escuela que en el autobús.

Para mi clase media malograda, llamada tercercermundista, luchar contra los avatares cotidianos eso siempre es resistir.

Michelle María Gómez Álvarez

Resist the Quotidian

My twisted eyes resist the screams of my mother
for the lack of money, the absence of my father,
inhabiting grandfather's room.
They resist my father, wrapped up in his quarrelsome
    alcoholism.
I resist studying physics and chemistry among the deafening
narcomusic of drugged neighbors, without prejudice.

I study between the land of my town and the asphalt
    of the city.
I live off scholarships, help from my uncles and a stoic
attitude to keep safe the old walnut, the fig tree,
    bougainvillea,
geraniums and roses that once cultivated the grandparents.
Trees and plants help me breathe and avoid terrible vices
in which young people of my age fall and never return from.

I will not smoke nicotine, I will not drink beer, nor whiskey,
    nor tequila;
much less will I know of synthetic addictions that kill the poor
and the miserable actors of television.

I study with stoicism to help nature and my generation.
I will not be a prey to fads or exorbitant consumerism.
Resist with a lot of faith, discipline and wise practice,
the same at school as on the bus.

For my ill-starred middle class, called third-world,
fighting the avatars of the quotidian, this is to resist.

Matheus Alves

Um Cordel Pro Valentão

Larga de ser covarde
E abaixa a tua mão,
Mulher é benção divina
A mais perfeita criação,
Não merece ser judiada
Muito menos maltratada,
Por seres sem coração.

Tenha plena consciência
Tu que estás a fazer,
Ao invés de bater nela
Faça amor, lhe dê prazer,
Pra que tanta violência
É preciso paciência,
Não a faça mais sofrer.

Irei passar um conselho
A você violentada,
Se você sofre e apanha
Não se contenha calada,
Bote a boca no trombone
E sua denúncia acione,
Mostre que tu és ousada.

A lei Maria da Penha
Vem punir o agressor
E mostrar que em mulher
Não se bate nem com flor
Mas lhe dar todo respeito
Aceitando o seu defeito
Seja ela como for.

Na briga de um casal
Se mete, sim, a colher,
Pois ela tem o direito
De ser bem o que quiser,
E se você ela amar
Vai sempre lhe apoiar,
Da cabeça até o pé.

Ame, apenas ame
De todo o coração,
Pois achamos que é certo
Andando na contramão,
Ela não quer ser agredida
Quer amar e ser ouvida,
Ter também sua atenção.

Matheus Alves

A String for the Bully

Stop being a coward
And lower your hand,
Woman is a divine blessing
The most perfect creation,
Doesn't deserve to be hurt
Much less abused,
By a heartless one.

Be mindful
Of what you are doing,
Don't hit her
Make love, give her pleasure,
Why so much violence
Patience is needed,
Don't make her suffer.

I'll give some advice
To you who are violated,
If you suffer and are hit
Do not keep silent,
Put your mouth on the trombone
And denounce,
Show that you are daring.

The Maria da Penha Law
Comes to punish the aggressor
And show that woman
We do not hit even with a flower
Give her all respect instead
Accepting her shortcomings
No matter what they are.

In the fight of a couple
We should of course meddle
Because she has the right
To be all that she wants,
And if you love her
You will always support her,
Top to toe.

Love, just love
Wholeheartedly
Because it is right
Swimming against the tide,
She doesn't want to be hurt
Want to be loved and be heard,
And have your attention as well.

Paloma Ximena Becerril Ramirez

Miedo

Tengo miedo
pero no que
frente a mi aparezca
un monstruo, un fantasma
o el mismo Lucifer.

No, eso ya no me asusta
tengo miedo de salir
y no regresar.

Tengo miedo de encontrarme
con una persona que acabe con mi destino,
tengo miedo de que alguien
con descontrol acabe con el mío.

Pero, lo que mas miedo me da
es lo que suceda a mi alrededor
si alguien acaba conmigo.

¿Por qué?
¿Por qué tengo que salir con miedo?
miedo de que alguien sucio y corrompido
me haga daño,

Miedo de que me chiflen,
que con una mirada sucia me destruya
que posen sus manos sobre mi cuerpo
sin yo quererlo.

¿Por qué?

Acaso no se supone
que somos humanos
seres que pensamos y razonados
y que solo imaginar hacerle daño a otro
debería parecernos una aberración.

Por eso tengo miedo
de salir y que
todo mundo conozca
el porque de mi día final.

Paloma Ximena Becerril Ramirez

Fear

I'm afraid
but not that
in front of me
a monster, a ghost
or Lucifer himself appears.

No, that does not scare me anymore.
I'm afraid to leave my home
and not return.

I'm afraid to meet
with a person who ends my destiny,
I'm afraid that someone
with lack of control, kills me.

Why?

Why do I have to leave home with fear,
afraid that someone dirty and corrupt
hurts me? Afraid that with a dirty look, they destroy me
that they put their hands on my body,
without me wanting it?

Why?

Aren't we supposed
to be rational human beings,
that only the thought of hurting another
would be an aberration?

That's why I am afraid to go out.

Priscila Oliveira Nascimento

Sementes de Luta

Milhares de rumores estou a ouvir
Sobre uma guerra que está por vir
Falta tolerância, respeito e educação
Pois têm como prioridade os tiros de canhão

A laicidade com seus dias contados
A desigualdade crescendo sem parar
O meio ambiente gritando por socorro
E a violência só tende a aumentar

E agora chegou nossa hora
Aos nossos antepassados temos que honrar
Porque se hoje temos a liberdade como direito
Foi conquista deles, que protestaram até sangrar

Juntos temos em nossas mãos o mundo
Juntos, não podem nos censurar
Dentro de cada um brada uma semente
Que em forma de luta vai germinar

Priscila Oliveira Nascimento

Seeds of Struggle

Thousands of rumors I'm listening
About a coming war
Lack of tolerance, respect and education
Because the cannon shots are their priority

Secularity with its days counted
Inequality growing non-stop
The environment screaming for help
And violence only increasing

And now it's our time
Our ancestors we must honor
If freedom today we have as a right
It was their conquest, who protested until bleeding

Together we have the world in our hands
Together, they cannot censor us.
Within each one of us a seed cries
Which in the shape of a struggle will germinate

Bean

Self-portrait

Jeanne Lainé

Depuis la Nuit des Temps

Femme, depuis la nuit des temps
Ta bouche fut cousue.
Femme, par tant de gens
Exhibée comme le fruit défendu.

Ton humanité bafouée
Ta parole dénigrée
Et, de ton corps dépossédée.

Mais ta pensée toujours tienne
Est la force qui te mène,
Qui te rappelle que la quête n'est pas vaine.

Femme, depuis la nuit des temps
Ton combat dans la pénombre
Femme, par tant de gens
Étouffé car il encombre.

Mais jamais elle n'a cessé
Ta quête de la liberté,
Jamais il n'a pu être effréné
Ton combat vers l'égalité.

Jeanne Lainé

Since the Dawn of Time

Woman, since the dawn of time
Your mouth was sewn.
Woman, by so many people
Exhibited as the forbidden fruit.

Your humanity trampled
Your word denigrated
And detached from your body.

But your thought always your own
Is the force that leads you,
Which reminds you that the quest is not in vain.

Woman, since the dawn of time
Your fight in the dark
Woman, by so many people
Stifled because it is inconvenient.

But it has never stopped
Your quest for freedom,
Never could it be slowed down
Your fight for equality.

Alexandre Joissains

Indolence Opaline

Béton se craquelle, une tige apparaît,
Un soupçon de vie nu sans tenue d'apparat.
Si le vent l'harcèle, son sang-froid transparaît,
Car brin d'herbe ingénu ne se soumettra pas.

On le met à genoux et le temps le piétine.
Dos courbé se dénoue car il ne se résigne.
De la chlorophylle comme seule résine
Mais l'herbe s'obstine, isolée, sans épines.

Pluie, grêle, orages, elle résiste à tout,
Sa détermination est son unique atout.
L'absence de rage, de peur, de haine itou,
Cette domination de la paix est partout.

Sans arme et violence, les cœurs des peuples battent.
Chaque herbe est un Homme, chaque âme est délicate.
Amour, indolence, s'éveillent, grondent et s'abattent
Sur chacun. En somme, notre force épate.

Alexandre Joissains

Indolence Opaline

Concrete is cracking, a stem appears,
A naked hint of life without adornment.
If the wind harasses it, its self-control is revealed,
Since a smart blade of grass will not bend.

We force it to its knees and time tramples it.
So it unfolds its back because it does not resign.
Chlorophyll as its only resin
But the grass is stubborn, alone, without thorns.

Rain, hail, storms, it resists everything,
Its determination is its only asset.
The absence of rage, fear, and hate,
This domination of peace is everywhere.

Without weapons and violence, the hearts of peoples fight.
Each blade of grass is a man, each soul is delicate.
Love, indolence, wake up, growl and fall
On every person. In short, our strength is amazing.

Audry Barré

Resistancialisme

Entends-tu au sein de la joie ce son de cor,
d'une guerre qui vola nos âmes et nos corps ?
Vois-tu les flammes brûler au coeur de Paris,
Laissant nos vies intactes mais pas nos esprits ?

Entends-tu ce mensonge qui viol le passé,
D'une France unie et qui a résistée ?
Vois-tu la mémoire des Étoiles enfumée,
Comme celle de la trahison partis en fumée

Entends-tu peurs et pleurs de notre Douce France
dont l'horreur s'abat sur les pures innocences ?
Vois-tu la purge et le sang innondant la terre,
Quand résistance devient folie rancunière ?

Audry Barré

Resistancialisme

Do you hear, mingled in the joy, this sound of the horn,
of a war that stole our souls and our bodies?
Do you see the flames burning in the heart of Paris,
Leaving our lives intact but not our minds?

Do you hear this lie that rapes the past,
Of a France united, and which resisted?
Do you see the smoky memory of the stars,
Like the one of betrayal gone up in smoke

Do you hear fears and tears of our sweet France
whose horror falls on pure innocence?
Do you see the purge and the blood flooding the earth,
When resistance becomes rancorous madness?

Trudy Pearce

Edited

I want the revised version of my life
looked through with a fine tooth comb
Just erase all my mistakes
Is that so much to ask?
No more judging friends, watching
waiting for my next screw up
No more expectations that I could never hope to meet
No more disappointed looks focused on my failures
Just let me succeed, I'm tired of being me

Homeless

Faith Victoria

Of a Tramp

Use your eyes,
Drag your sight
From daily life,
There's some in London
Who are lost in night.
Shivering, collapsed,
Trying to find
Some warmth in rags.
Who watch the dirty day
As on it drags.
While cars growl,
And filthy trains thunder,
Their happiness
Is completely under.
Distress engulfs,
It might be hard
To understand
Their deep despair.
They lost the certainty,
That they would win,
And so, like holes
They have completely
Caved in.

Tree Stumps

Natalie Rovello

Making Maps

On november 8th, 2016
(*a date which will live in infamy*)
I sat like a child on my bed
I had always thought myself an artist,
So I took a pen and drew a map -
Every line
Of every state
I drew my home
And my family's home.
My father's side arrived in 1750
They crossed the Gap before Daniel Boone
My ancestors fought In the wars of their eras,
And so did my father and brothers.
My mother's side arrived in 1950
They built lives
They built cities
They built corner stores and restaurants and
    dairy companies and car washes.
I made a map of the United States,
I made a map of my family tree,
I made a map of myself
And I colored it piece by piece
As the results came in
I colored it red
Like a flame, like a blood splatter,
I sat like a child on my bed
And I cried

Hector Manuel Orreaga Ramirez

El Sentido de la Vida

Algun dia todo tendrá sentido,
por ahora ríete ante la confusión,
sonríe a través de las lágrimas
y sigue recordando que todo
pasa por una razón.

Hector Manuel Orreaga Ramirez

The Meaning of Life

Someday everything will make sense,
for now, laugh at the confusion,
Smile through tears
and keep remembering that everything
happens for a reason.

Alex Perez

The Truth

I, I am a black male
The truth
I am a black male who can't be overpowered again
The truth
Your probably thinking
What is this kid thinking he wasn't there back then
The truth
But the thing is I'm Haitian
Sap pasé (wassup)
My ancestors t'ap boulé
(Heating up)
Picking sugar cane to make who we are eating fried
Plaintains as the Haitians

Dana Abou-Diab, 15, is from Arkansas with a passion for science and zoology. She enjoys the meaning behind certain poems and how they express emotion. She also really enjoys everything Batman and DC Comics.

Joss Aiken, 14, a nonbinary, cat-loving Potterhead, lives in Connecticut. Originally from the UK, they plan to return there for university. Joss spends a lot of their time advocating for equity, and the rest working hard on the Shakespeare play they are acting in, their schoolwork, poetry, cats, and other hobbies.

Michelle María Gómez Álvarez, 18, studies Engineering at the University. She won the first prize in the poetry contest of Tepotzotlan, Mexico, in 2018. The inspiration for her poetry comes from her observations of the socio-economic difficulties in her life as a daughter and a student, which are similar to those of the youth in many other countries who struggle to have a career, in spite of all the difficulties that surround them.

Matheus Alves, 14, is in 9th grade. He loves reading and writing poetry. His dream is to study Spanish and English Literature in College. His love for writing started when he was a semifinalist in Portuguese Language Olympiad Competition. Since then he has never stopped writing.

Bhagyashree Barman, 17, is an Indian currently staying in Assam. He recently completed his schooling and loves to dance and write poems. He is a big fan of literature and reading is his favourite leisure time activity. He has been writing poetry since he was in 4th grade and continued doing so till date. Other than writing poems, he writes short stories as well..

Audry Barré, 18, has been writing poetry since she was 10 years old. A French student, who works in a literary classroom, she loves to play with words to be beautiful, to amuse or denounce.

Drizzle Bayer, 14, is half Turkish, half Brazilian, and currently lives in Macau, China. A lot of the inspiration for her poetry and writing is drawn from her real-life experiences and issues that she feels aren't spoken about enough in the media and the world in general.

Elizabeth Bowling, 15, is a freshman at Crawfordsville High School who loves writing, reading, watching 80s movies and TV shows, playing with her siblings, and singing along with Broadway musicals at the top of her lungs. She thanks the Social Justice Club for this opportunity and her family for their support.

Rayna Bowman, 15, first started writing poetry this year. She enjoys the power words can have. Not only does she write poetry, she also plays soccer and volleyball. She believes poetry is a great way to connect with people on another level.

Laila Carter, 17, a writer in Baltimore, Maryland. Currently she is a literary arts student at George Washington Carver Center for the Arts and Technology. Laila Carter explores all genres of writing but adores poetry the most. She is inspired by all things mundane and beautiful.

Mion Charity is a 9th grader from Missouri. She loves all aspects of the fine arts especially writing and painting. Her inspiration for writing is nature and relationships. She loves nature because of its beauty and complexity, much like relationships.

Dominique Cuningkin, 17, is a junior in high school. She found a love for writing in Kindergarten and has been doing it ever since. She's been inspired to use her gift to hopefully one day spread her opinions throughout the world in a way that everybody can relate to. She is currently working on a collection of poetry inspired by the Social Justice theme and a novel meant to inspire many young minority females.

R'keria Davis, 17, is a high school senior who has an infatuation with animals, music, poetry, and books. Her works have received recognition at both the local and national levels. She plans to work in environmental policy and continue her writing journey.

Krishi Desai, 16, is a junior at Bergen County Academis in New Jersey. When Krishi was younger, she used to ask her mom to tell her the same bedtime stories so often that she memorized all of them. One of Krishi's favorite authors is Edgar Allan Poe. Her poem was also published by The Visible Poetry Project and Live Poets Society of New Jersey.

Shivani Deshmukh, 17, is a robust nationalist. 5 years old self-proclaimed geek. Chocolate addict. Loves dogs and cats equally. Intentionally watches tear- jerking movies. Owns a playlist full of manifold songs. A hopeless dreamer.

Taylor Drummer, 18, attends Lincoln College Preparatory Academy as a Senior. The inspiration for this poem emanates from being observant of African Americans and elaborating on how life is already hard on them for being black and how they are deprived of the resources necessary to evolve.

Molly Duke, 17, is a student at Olathe North High-school and is a fanatic for writing controversial poetry. For this poem she *simply wanted to raise my voice against the issue of sexual harassment, specifically the dismissal of it by those in authority.*

Sophia Gotham, 14, is an 8th grader from Kansas City, Missouri. She loves to sing, make art, read, act, and swim.

William Graham, 15, is also know as Mr. Insanity. Writing is his absolute life. He has been doing it ever since he could pick up the pencil. *It's simply my blissful escape from this human world.*

Augustus Hoff, 15, is a Sophomore at Pasco High School, who always strives to be the change he wishes to see in the world. That is why he is an active participant in sports, clubs, and anything else he can find to make a positive change on people.

Alexandre Joissains, 16, lives in France. He started writing two years ago when he was 14. During those two years, he wrote around 200 poems, and a song for a friend. He would love to become a songwriter.

Katherine Kallas, 16, is a junior at St. Teresa's Academy in Kansas City, Missouri. She has loved poetry from a young age and has started writing some of her own in the past couple of years. Poetry has been an outlet for her to express herself and has helped her through some hard times. *In a world where young people's voices are often overlooked, poetry gives us a chance to share our opinions and feelings with a broader audience.*

Nataly Kazzi, 17, wants people reading her poem to be able to get over typical Clichés women are distinguished as. *We deserve to live in a world where people don't see us as metaphors and objects or even weak, but see us as strong, beautiful, independent human beings.*

Rehma Khan, 16, lives in Karachi, Pakistan. She studies at the City School and is in grade 9. Her favorite poets include Matthew Arnold, William Wordsworth and Alfred Tennyson.

Ashley Kim, 17, is a junior at Bergen County Academies in New Jersey. She has won numerous prizes for her writing, including publication in Just Poetry's 2018 winter issue, gold, silver, and honorable mention keys in the Scholastic Art and Writing Awards, and was a winner of the Walt Whitman Poetry Contest. Her poem "Foreign Tongues" has also been published in AMERICAN HIGH SCHOOL POETS "JUST POETRY!!!" the NATIONAL POETRY QUARTERLY (2018 winter issue).

Jeanna Laine, 17, attends high school in Quimper, France. She chose to write about feminism because *even though we are in the twenty-first century, women everywhere in the world still fight against inequalities and for their rights.*

An avid flutist and people-watcher, **Joanna Lau,** 18, lives in New York and is a senior in Herricks High School's English Scholars (Creative Writing) Program. Her poetry and creative nonfiction have received a Gold Medal and four Gold Keys in Scholastic Art & Writing Awards.

Jasmine Li, 16, is a student at Lower Merion High School. She's a master procrastinator and a self-diagnosed skincare addict. Jasmine has been writing amateur poetry since seventh grade but this is her first publication ever! Find more of her poems on Instagram: @vanilla.lune.

Ileana Viridiana Romero Lopez, 16, was born in Norristown, Pennsylvania, but due to psychological problems had to move to Mexico. She always liked reading but also found out how much she likes writing what she feels. *This poem I wrote while I was thinking about how none of us know how much time we have left.*

Minerva Macarrulla, 17, is a high school senior from Brooklyn whose passions include poetry, environmentalism, dance, and intersecting social issues. Minerva has received four gold keys from the Scholastic Writing Awards and recently won a spot on UrbanWord NYC's 2019 slam team. Minerva plans to attend Oberlin College in the Fall.

Ava Minu-Sepehr, 17, writes from her experiences as an Iranian-American woman. Her father and his family were forced to flee Iran in the 1979 Iranian Revolution, and she tries to convey the impact of this displacement on her identity and language. She also enjoys spending time with her sister and friends.

Since he was very young, **Pablo Montalvão**, 17, was in love with the poems his father, Palmerindo Sousa, wrote. He passed away when Pablo was 6 years old *but I inherited from him my love for words.* You can find Pablo's poems on his blog: www.pablomontalvao.blogspot.com

Priscila Oliveira Nascimento, 16, is from Brazil, a country rich in culture which has been passed down from one generation to another. She has been writing short stories since she was a child but it was poetry that rescued and gave meaning to her words.

Sidra Nizami, 18, is from New Delhi, India. She is a student at The Pinnacle School. After graduating she aspires to study English Literature for her higher education and pursue a career as an English literature lecturer in a well-known University.

Poetry has always been a sense of identification for **Rachel Otero**, 17. She has learned a lot about herself through her writing as well as about the world. With her writing she hopes to inspire a parallel feeling between her words and the reader's own experiences.

Trudy Pearce, 14, was born in Nottingham, UK, but has spent most of her life in China. She is a student at the School of the Nations, Macau, and writes poems to get her emotions down on paper and share them. She especially likes exploring new places and feminism.

Alex Perez, 14, started writing poems in sixth grade as a way to express himself and his emotions. As a young man, it was hard to show his feelings and writing did that.

Hector Manuel Orreaga Ramirez, 17, was born in Peru and lives now in Spain where he attends technical high school. He likes social poetry through which he can advocate peace and help for the most vulnerable.

Paloma Ximena Becerril Ramirez, 13, was inspired to write this poem by seeing, daily, abuses on the news and hearing about them from her friends. These abuses, moreover, constitute what people experience in Mexico.

Chloe Jane Rosenstock, 17, lives in Los Angeles, California, and has been writing poetry since she was 13. She uses writing as her main form of expression. She cannot imagine what her adolescence would have been without poetry.

Natalie Rovello, 16, is a sophomore at St. Teresa's Academy. Her poem Making Maps won a Gold Key in the Scholastic Writing Awards and will also be featured in the literary publication Elementia. She takes a lot of pride and inspiration from her family history, and how that intersects with both her personal life and current events.

Thayse Souza dos Santos, 15, lives off dreams. They keep her days lighter and full of color. She aspires to be a great writer, get to learn about new cultures and travel around the world, captivating the hearts with her words. She thanks her godmother and teacher, Rita Freire, and her school coordinator, Katia Valmont, for the opportunity they gave her to participate in this contest. *I dedicate my poem to all my friends who believed in me.*

Giselly Kamily de Jesus Santos, 13, loves reading and to express herself through poetry. She dreams of traveling the world with the aim of being a better person every day. She would like to thank her Portuguese teacher, Rita Freire, and her school coordinator, Katia Valmont, for this wonderful opportunity to write and to show the world the beauty that blooms from within her soul.

Katherine Vandermel, 16, strives to create meaning with the strongest weapon: words. When she is not writing, she is reading and refreshing herself with the news of the world. Katherine is so glad to share her work with others in this anthology.

Narine Verdiyan, 16, is an Armenian poet who resides in Ann Arbor, Michigan. They go to Washtenaw Technical Middle College and are pursuing an associate degree in Liberal Arts. They love animals, plants, and writing short stories.

Faith Emily Victoria, 13, was born in New Zealand. She now lives in England and attends St Margarets Secondary School in Bushey, where she pesters teachers every day for news of more writing competitions. Her favorite subjects are English, Drama and History.

Somya Wadhwa, 18, loves conversations over a cup of coffee. She likes to believe in people, and decipher everything trivial. She will always say yes to swinging in the park or watching Gilmore Girls. If lost, look for the nearest book store.

Rialin S. Yasay, 16, is a grade 11 student from the Philippines, best know for writing poems that inspire the readers. With her poem entitled "Weapons in the War of Life", she won the first-place prize in a poetry writing contest which was held during the Teachers' Month 2018

This project was made possible, in part, by generous support from the Osage Arts Community.

Osage Arts Community provides temporary time, space and support for the creation of new artistic works in a retreat format, serving creative people of all kinds — visual artists, composers, poets, fiction and nonfiction writers. Located on a 152-acre farm in an isolated rural mountainside setting in Central Missouri and bordered by ¾ of a mile of the Gasconade River, OAC provides residencies to those working alone, as well as welcoming collaborative teams, offering living space and workspace in a country environment to emerging and mid-career artists. For more information, visit us at www.osageac.org

www.ingramcontent.com/pod-product-compliance
Lightning Source LLC
Chambersburg PA
CBHW041312110526
44591CB00022B/2894